America's
National Parks

America's
National Parks

CHARTWELL
BOOKS

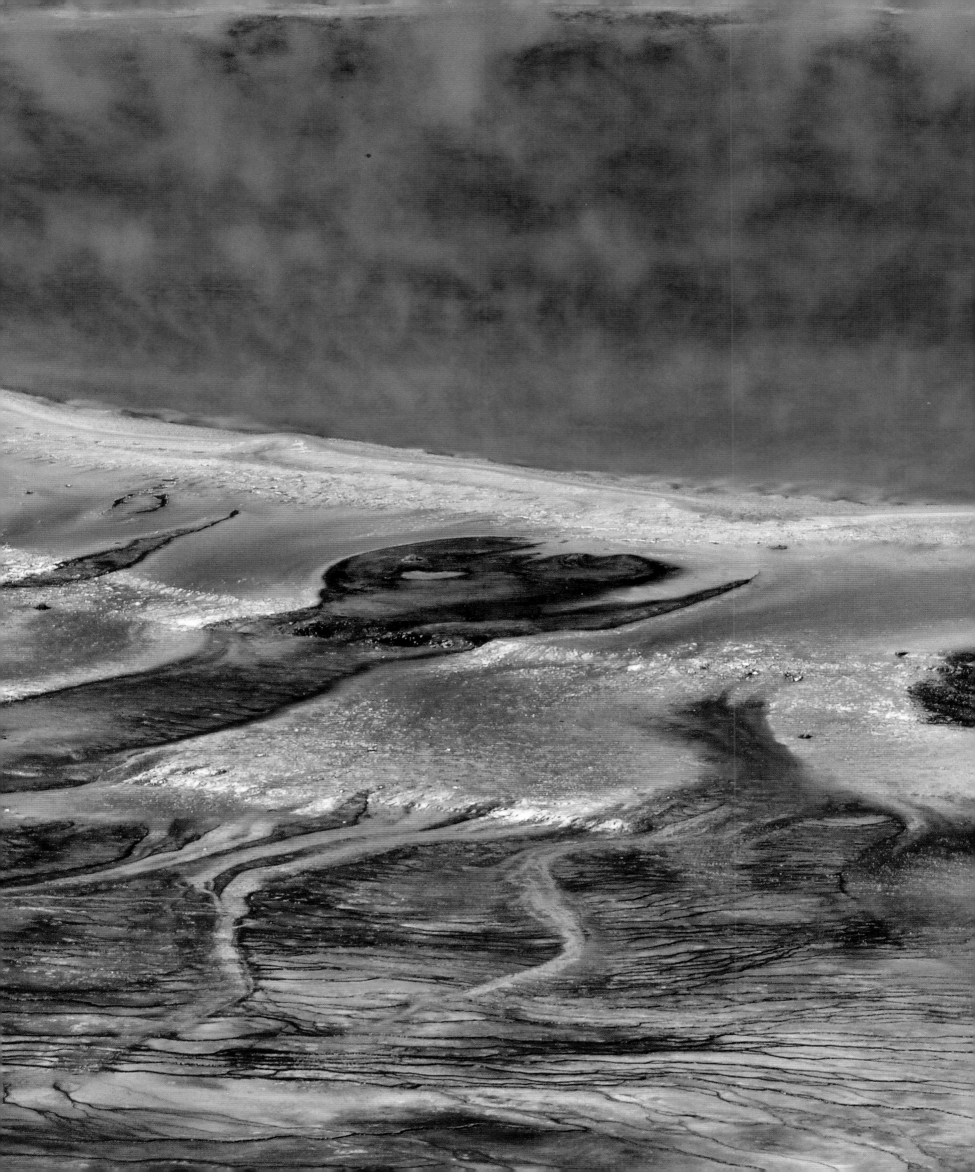

P. 2: A STUNNING LANDSCAPE TYPICAL OF THE AMERICAN WEST CAN BE GLIMPSED THROUGH THE CENTER OF THE DELICATE ARCH ROCK FORMATION. ARCHES NATIONAL PARK, UTAH.

PP. 4-5: ROUTE 163 RUNS BETWEEN THE HILLS AND MESAS OF MONUMENT VALLEY. THE RED ROCK FORMATIONS RESULTED FROM THE EARTH'S CRUST MOVING AND CRACKING.

PP. 6-7: GREAT SMOKY MOUNTAINS NATIONAL PARK IS ONE OF THE MOST POPULAR PARKS IN THE UNITED STATES. THE SMOKIES, SOME OF THE TALLEST MOUNTAINS IN THE AMERICAS, WERE NAMED FOR THE SMOKY-LOOKING FOG THAT SURROUNDS THEM MUCH OF THE TIME.

PP. 8-9: GRAND PRISMATIC SPRING, THE LARGEST HOT SPRING IN YELLOWSTONE NATIONAL PARK, WYOMING, RESEMBLES AN ABSTRACT PAINTING.

PP. 10-11: THE CALIFORNIA DESERT IS A VARIED, ALMOST SURREAL LANDSCAPE WITH PLANT AND ANIMAL LIFE FOUND IN FEW OTHER PLACES IN THE WORLD. DUE TO THE EXTREME HEAT AND DRY CLIMATE, THE DESERT COMES TO LIFE AFTER DARK. AS NIGHT FALLS, FROGS CROAK, COYOTES HOWL, AND HORNED OWLS HOOT. RACETRACK PLAYA, DEATH VALLEY NATIONAL PARK, CALIFORNIA.

OPPOSITE: ZABRISKIE POINT IN DEATH VALLEY NATIONAL PARK IS PART OF AN AREA KNOWN AS THE "BADLANDS" BECAUSE NO PLANTS GROW IN ITS DRY, SALINE SOIL—SEDIMENT FROM FURNACE CREEK, WHICH DRIED UP FIVE MILLION YEARS AGO. IN THE EARLY TWENTIETH CENTURY, CHRISTIAN BREVOORT ZABRISKIE WAS VICE PRESIDENT AND GENERAL MANAGER OF THE PACIFIC COAST BORAX COMPANY, WHICH MINED BORAX IN DEATH VALLEY, CALIFORNIA.

Pp. 14-15: Inspiration Point offers spectacular views of the dramatic rock formations in Bryce Canyon National Park, known as hoodoos. The Paiute tribe called them "red rocks standing like men in a bowl-shaped recess."

Opposite: Horseshoe Bend is not technically part of a national park, but many visitors to the parks in Arizona stop to view it. This sharp twist in the Colorado River is part of the Glen Canyon National Recreation Area, about five miles (eight kilometers) from Glen Canyon Dam and Lake Powell. The brightly colored water contrasts with the muted red rocks.

Pp. 18-19: Grizzly bears hunt salmon in Brooks Falls, Katmai National Park, Alaska. Alaska remains a stronghold for grizzly bears and is their ideal habitat.

CONTENTS

INTRODUCTION

The enormous size of the United States—nearly 3.8 million square miles, or more than nine million square kilometers—makes it hard to generalize about the country. The fifty states are very varied. Just consider the vast difference between the climate of snowy Alaska, to the far northwest, and warm Hawaii, miles from the West Coast in the Pacific Ocean. The country's national parks reflect that diversity. This collection provides an overview and focuses on highlights, but it is not a comprehensive list.

There are more than 400 areas protected under the national park system of the United States, comprising more than 80 million acres (32 million hectares) of land in forty-nine of the fifty states. Of those, fifty-eight are officially designated as national parks. Not all parks are equal in the eyes of the people, however. The best-known national parks in the system have been photographed so often that they are as famous as any painting or work of sculpture—they are masterpieces in their own right.

Some of these protected areas have been pristinely preserved over centuries. They appear today as they did during the time of the pioneers, when settlers pushed further west in search of land and raw materials, creating ranches, roads, railways, and dams as they went.

It was a desire to safeguard this land against such human settlement that led the U.S. government to create a network of protected areas,

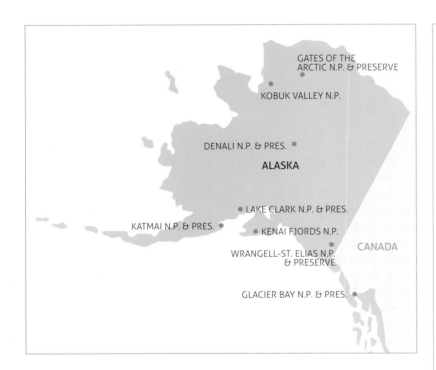

which evolved into today's national parks. Many forward-thinking figures understood that such land was a limited resource to be carefully guarded. East Coast writers such as Ralph Waldo Emerson, Henry David Thoreau, and Walt Whitman believed nature had the power to purify the human. "Now I see the secret of making the best person: it is to grow in the open air and to eat and sleep with the earth," Whitman wrote in "Song of the Open Road." In the West, naturalist and writer John Muir, one of the founders of the Sierra Club, the oldest and largest environmental organization in the United States, spoke forcefully in support of protecting the wilderness. He believed man could co-exist with nature without depleting its resources.

The modern paradox in all this is that preserving natural places almost always involves opening them up to visitors, which means these parks are now equipped with hotels, roads, walkways, and campgrounds.

In 1872, President Ulysses S. Grant first conceived of a national park and signed the law establishing Yellowstone National Park, located in both Montana and Wyoming, as a protected area that would be preserved for future generations.

Several new parks were added in the late nineteenth century: Yosemite (1890), Sequoia (1890), and Mount Rainier (1899). In 1903, President Theodore Roosevelt made a big push to create more reserves, parks, and national monuments, and the 1906 Antiquities Act secured protection for Native American archeological sites, including Mesa Verde and the Grand Canyon. The National Park Service was created in 1916 under the direction of Stephen Mather, and then in the 1930s President Franklin Delano Roosevelt added another fifty locations to its purview, which created hundreds of jobs for road workers and construction workers during the Great Depression. After World War II, the National Park Service continued to grow, and in 1966 the National Historic Preservation Act added to its administrative and legal powers. Expansion is ongoing to this day. The Great Sand Dunes National Park and Preserve became official in 2004, yet another building block in a system designed to preserve the natural splendor that is in so many ways the essence of the American spirit.

Map Legend

●   National Park

------   State Border

▩   United States

WEST COAST

The West Coast of the United States boasts beautiful coastlines, arid deserts, and forests filled with age-old trees. In short, it offers a wide range of spectacular nature. The three states on the Pacific Ocean are filled with truly beautiful national parks.

Washington state, which borders Canada to the north, is known for its damp, rainy climate. The state has three national parks: Mount Rainier National Park, North Cascades National Park, and Olympic National Park. Mount Rainier is actually a volcano more than 13,000 feet (4,000 meters) high. Its peak is covered in ice and snow year-round, while the slopes are warmer and greener, with dense forests and meadows. Naturalist John Muir wrote of the area, "If in the making of the West, Nature had what we call parks in mind—places for rest, inspiration, and prayers—this Rainier region must surely be one of them." Olympic National Park near Seattle is often described as three parks in one, as it encompasses three widely varied ecosystems: the untamed Pacific coastline, glacial mountains, and one of the world's most beautiful rainforests, including Hoh Rainforest, where moss-covered trees stretch out their long limbs to create mystical scenery.

To the south, in Oregon, a crater that formed due to the eruption of Mount Mazama is now Crater Lake. This crystalline body of water has lent its name to the park. The lake is almost 2,000 feet (600 meters) deep and has rocky walls and a small island. It is truly magical.

California, the most populous state in the country, not only includes big cities such as Los Angeles, San Francisco, and San Diego, but a large share of the country's natural beauty, much of it protected as part of the state's eight parks. Joshua Tree National Park, with the low Colorado Desert and the high Mojave Desert, was named for the trees native to this area. Death

Valley National park offers surreal views.

Amid the Sierra Nevada mountains sits Yosemite National Park, a treasure chest of rock formations, waterfalls, and sequoia forests and considered one of the standouts of the national park system. Yosemite is paradise for hikers and rock climbers and attracts millions of visitors every year.

South of Yosemite, Sequoia National Park and Kings Canyon National Park are home, respectively, to giant sequoias and one of the deepest canyons in the United States. Farther north, Redwood National Park, Lassen Volcanic National Park, and Channel Islands National Park are as varied as they are splendid.

LEFT: YOSEMITE FALLS DROPS MORE THAN HALF A MILE (ALMOST A FULL KILOMETER) IN THREE DIRECTIONS. THE FALLS ARE AT THEIR PEAK IN SPRING, WHEN RAINWATER FILLS THEM TO CAPACITY. IN THE SUMMER THEY SLOW TO A TRICKLE. YOSEMITE NATIONAL PARK, CALIFORNIA.

RIGHT: MOVING ROCKS, ALSO KNOWN AS SAILING STONES OR SLIDING ROCKS, ARE LOCATED ON RACETRACK PLAYA, A LAKE IN DEATH VALLEY, CALIFORNIA. THE ROCKS MOVE FOR THREE TO FOUR YEARS AND LEAVE TRAILS UP TO A YARD LONG AND A FEW INCHES DEEP. THIS PHENOMENON LEFT OBSERVERS SCRATCHING THEIR HEADS FOR MANY YEARS, BUT TODAY SCIENTISTS BELIEVE THAT WIND CAUSED AS THIN SHEETS OF ICE FORM UNDER THE STONES PUSHES THEM ALONG. DEATH VALLEY NATIONAL PARK, CALIFORNIA.

OLYMPIC NATIONAL PARK

Olympic National Park in Washington was declared a national monument in 1909 and a national park in 1938. It is 1,442 square miles (3,734 square kilometers) and consists of three distinct natural environments: the Pacific coastline, the mountains, and the eastern temperate rainforest and drier rainforest to the west.

The rainforest on the western side of the park is rich in plant life, including Sitka spruce, giant thuya, maple trees, and hemlock. The trees grow to dizzying heights and can be up to sixty-five feet (twenty meters) in circumference. Many are covered heavily in moss and lichen.

The coastline in this park is an irregularly shaped beach that alternates between sand and rocks and runs alongside a strip of woods.

The Hoh and Quileute Native Americans live at the mouths of the two rivers of the same name, the former near the town of La Push.

The Olympic Mountains are the centerpiece of the park. The mountainsides are covered in glaciers. The largest is the Hoh Glacier, which is three miles (almost five kilometers) long.

The eastern mountains are drier, as they are sheltered from the rain on the western side. The tallest peak in this mountain range is Mount Deception, which rises nearly 8,000 feet (2,400 meters) in the air.

Olympic National Park is also home to many animal species, including the Olympic marmot, believed to exist only here. The park is also home to the largest herd of Roosevelt elk in the United States.

In 1976, UNESCO designated the park an International Biosphere Reserve; in 1981 it was added to the list of UNESCO World Heritage Sites.

In 1988, further protection was granted to 95 percent of the park when it was designated Olympic Wilderness.

Pp. 24-25: Hoh Rainforest in Olympic National Park is one of the largest temperate rainforests in the world. The heavy rains and generally damp environment foster impressive growth. Many of the trees that grow here—including subalpine fir and Canadian fir—reach gigantic size, with trunks up to twenty-three feet (seven meters) in diameter. Moss and vines grow thickly as well, forming curtains that hang down from the trees. Look closely and you can see woodpeckers, bluebirds, hummingbirds, and finch flying among them. Olympic National Park, Washington.

Pp. 26-27: Hurricane Ridge is the highest spot in the park that can be reached by car. A winding road rises almost 5,000 feet (1,500 meters) above sea level in just seventeen miles (twenty-seven kilometers). Hiking, skiing, and snowboarding can be enjoyed year-round, as can the views of the glaciers on Mount Carrie and Mount Olympus. Olympic National Park, Washington.

Left: In the rainier western side of the park, the Sol Duc Falls mark the start of the Seven Lakes Basin Loop, a nineteen-mile (twenty-eight kilometer) path that leads to the Sol Duc Hot Springs and the Bogachiel River. The area is lush with wildlife and plant life as well. Olympic National Park, Washington.

Above: Just south of the town of La Push are three coastal gems: First, Second, and Third Beach are adjacent, but separated by promontories and cliffs. The small islands off the coast provide the ideal habitat for birds such as seagulls, oyster catchers, petrels, and cormorants. Second Beach, Olympic National Park, Washington.

Pp. 30-31: Rock formations and small islands, often robed in thick fog, make the fifty-seven-mile (ninety-two-kilometer) coastline in this area quite evocative. Ruby Beach, Olympic National Park, Washington.

MOUNT RAINIER NATIONAL PARK

Mount Rainier National Park was created in 1899 and declared a national monument in 1997. It includes 370 square miles (957 square kilometers) of land. Mount Rainier, a volcano, dominates the scene at 14,410 feet (4,390 meters) above sea level. This is the tallest mountain in the Cascades and the fifth tallest in the United States. On clear days, it can be seen from miles away, right up to its icy white peak.

The Indians who once lived in this area called the mountain *tahoma*, which means "large mountain with power to make thunder and lightning." One of the largest glaciers in the United States can be found at the top of Mount Rainier; its meadows and forests are home to thousands of different plant and animal species.

Indeed, the whole park has richly diverse wildlife: squirrels, pikas, mountain lions, bears, bobcats, beavers, foxes, and mountain goats. Bird species in the park include mountain chickadees, Steller's jays, Clark's nutcrackers, blackbirds, and bald eagles, as well as grouse and peregrine falcons.

Paradise on the slopes of Mount Rainier is one of the most popular areas in the park. The Paradise Inn was built here in 1916.

Paradise is also home to the park's main information office, Jackson Visitor Center, but the area is best known for its gorgeous views and wildflower meadows. Legend has it that when explorer and settler James Longmire's daughter first saw the valley spread before her, she exclaimed, "Oh, what a paradise!"

Longmire's Medical Springs is located in the Longmire area. Longmire and his family used these springs from 1888 to 1889. The original buildings have been converted into a museum where visitors can learn local history. Sunrise, which is 6,400 feet (about 1,950 meters) above sea level, is the highest spot in the park that can be reached by car. It is lush with wildflower meadows and on clear days offers a full view of Mount Rainier, Emmons Glacier, and many other peaks in the Cascades.

Paradoxically, Mount Rainier was named not for a mountaineer, but for a sailor, Admiral Peter Rainier. His good friend Captain George Vancouver first saw the snowy volcano in 1792 and named it in his honor.

OPPOSITE: MOUNT RAINIER IS A VOLCANO THAT REACHES 14,410 FEET (4,390 METERS) ABOVE SEA LEVEL. THE PEAK IS SNOW-COVERED YEAR-ROUND BY A SNOW SHIELD THAT RUNS DOWNWARD TO FORM SEVENTY GLACIERS. MOUNT RAINIER NATIONAL PARK IS 370 SQUARE MILES (957 SQUARE KILOMETERS) OF DENSE RED CEDAR AND DOUGLAS FIR. MYRTLE FALLS, IN THE FOREGROUND, IS IN THE SOUTHWEST AREA OF THE PARK AND IS ONE OF ITS MANY STUNNING SIGHTS.

Pp. 34-35: Reflection Lake, Mount Rainier National Park. The lake perfectly frames a reflection of all of Mount Rainier.

Above: Paradise, on the south side of Mount Rainier, is the most popular area of the park. It includes Paradise Valley and Paradise Glacier. Travel one of the many hiking paths that start here and you can enjoy nature without ever losing sight of the snowy peak of Mount Rainier.

Right: Red fox, Mount Rainier National Park.

REDWOOD NATIONAL PARK

Redwood National Park extends 280 miles (455 kilometers) along the Pacific coast. It is named for the hulking sequoia redwood trees native to California and Oregon.

The park was created in 1968 to protect the trees in the area. While at one time there were two million acres (810,000 hectares) of redwoods in northern California and southern Oregon, only 4 percent of that survives today. About half of that surviving land falls within park boundaries.

Naturally, the trees are the main attraction in this park, and they are impressive. Redwoods can grow up to more than 300 feet (ninety meters) in height. But the park is full of other attractions as well: beautiful pristine beaches, meadows, streams, and forests full of Douglas fir, Sitka spruce, and hemlock trees offer shelter to a wide array of animals. Roosevelt elk graze in the meadows, while seals and sea lions inhabit the coastline and salmon and trout swim in the rivers and streams.

THIS PAGE: A MALE ROOSEVELT ELK STANDS AND STARES. THESE ANIMALS CAN WEIGH 1,000 POUNDS (450 KILOGRAMS) OR MORE. THEY GRAZE IN THE MEADOWS AND CAN OFTEN BE GLIMPSED FROM THE ROAD. LIKE MANY OF THE ANIMALS NATIVE TO THIS AREA, THEIR NUMBERS HAVE DWINDLED OVER THE YEARS.

P. 39: ANCIENT SEQUOIA TREES ARE THE FOCAL POINT OF THIS RESERVE, WHICH LIES ALONG AN EXTENSIVE COASTAL AREA. REDWOOD NATIONAL PARK, CALIFORNIA.

Opposite: Fern Canyon is a narrow dirt path in Home Creek. The steep rock faces here are covered in moss and ferns. Among the amphibians that make their home here is the Pacific giant salamander. Redwood National Park, California.

YOSEMITE NATIONAL PARK

Yosemite Valley is often conflated with Yosemite National Park, but in reality the valley is only eight miles (thirteen kilometers) long, and while it is indubitably lovely, it accounts for only 3 percent of the total area of the park.

The confusion is understandable, because the numbers related to this park are mind-boggling. Yosemite National Park is 1,169 square miles (3,027 square kilometers). Though the number of visitors is also enormous, the park is large enough that it maintains the feel of open wilderness. Rock formations, soaring peaks, and rushing waterfalls continue to exist as they always have, unaltered by the tourists who flock to view them.

The park is home to black bears. Many of the bears in the park have become accustomed to humans and barely seem to register their presence. They are, however, attracted to the smell of human food and often wander into campgrounds and approach cars in search of something to eat. The park rules require that all foodstuffs and any garbage be tightly sealed in order to discourage such encounters.

The park was created in 1890 and is home to some of the world's tallest mountains. Half Dome stands more than 4,730 feet (1,440 meters) above the valley below. This rock formation, created by movements in ice and deposits in the valley, has become a symbol of Yosemite, along with its fellow rock formation, El Capitan. At 7,575 feet (2,300

OPPOSITE: HALF DOME STANDS MORE THAN 4,730 FEET (1,440 METERS) ABOVE THE VALLEY FLOOR AND IS A SYMBOL OF THE PARK. YOSEMITE NATIONAL PARK, CALIFORNIA.

meters), El Capitan is one of the largest granite rock formations in the world.

John Muir (1838-1914) was an early explorer of Yosemite Valley, and he collected his impressions and experiences in his autobiography, *My First Summer in the Sierra*. He wrote of the joy inspired in him by the great beauty of nature: "Probably more free sunshine falls on this majestic range than on any other in the world I've ever seen or heard of. It has the brightest weather, brightest glacier-polished rocks, the greatest abundance of colorful spray from its glorious waterfalls, the brightest forests of silver firs and silver pines, more starshine, moonshine, and perhaps more crystal-shine than any other mountain chain, and its countless mirror lakes, having more light poured into them, glow and spangle most. And how glorious the shining after the short summer showers and after frosty nights when the morning sunbeams are pouring through the crystals on the grass and pine needles, and how ineffably spiritually fine is the morning-glow on the mountaintops and the alpenglow of evening. Well may the Sierra be named, not the Snowy Range, but the Range of Light."

PP. 44-45: YOSEMITE VALLEY, SEEN FROM TUNNEL VIEW, OFFERS SOME OF THE PARK'S MOST BREATHTAKING VIEWS OF SLOPES, WATERFALLS, AND ROCK FORMATIONS. BRIDALVEIL FALL, RIGHT, IS NOTHING SHORT OF SPECTACULAR. IT IS 617 FEET (190 METERS) HIGH AND SITS OPPOSITE EL CAPITAN, ONE OF THE WORLD'S LARGEST ROCK FORMATIONS. HALF DOME IS VISIBLE IN THE BACKGROUND. YOSEMITE NATIONAL PARK, CALIFORNIA.

OPPOSITE: VERNAL FALL ON THE MERCED RIVER IS 317 FEET (96 METERS) LONG. YOSEMITE NATIONAL PARK, CALIFORNIA.

PP. 48-49: THE AREA, SEEN HERE IN WINTER, IS STUNNING YEAR-ROUND. YOSEMITE VALLEY, CALIFORNIA.

OPPOSITE: EL CAPITAN LOOMS OVER YOSEMITE VALLEY WITH A VERTICAL DROP OF 7,575 FEET (2,300 METERS) DOWN TO SEA LEVEL. ITS SLICK FACE IS KNOWN AS THE NOSE AND POSES A GREAT CHALLENGE TO ROCK CLIMBERS. EL CAPITAN WAS NAMED BY THE MARIPOSA BATTALION, WHICH EXPLORED THE VALLEY IN 1851, AND IS THE SPANISH TRANSLATION OF ITS NATIVE NAME, TOTOCKAHNOOLAH. ROCK CLIMBERS AFFECTIONATELY REFER TO IT AS "EL CAP."

SEQUOIA NATIONAL PARK AND KINGS CANYON NATIONAL PARK

In Sequoia National Park, in the southern Sierra Nevada, nature seems to have heeded the challenge to go big or go home: Amid some of the most colossal mountains in the country, the world's largest trees, sequoias, have found their ideal habitat. Scottish-born naturalist John Muir, the driving force behind creation of this park, wrote, "Every tree seemed religious and conscious of the presence of God." The sole enemy of these giants, which can grow up to 260 feet (80 meters) in height, is man, who since the pioneer days has been knocking them down to clear land for mines, roads, ranches, and pastures. Today these giant trees are protected in the park—which was created in 1890 and has been expanded several times. Sequoia National

Park borders Kings Canyon National Park, created in 1940. Kings Canyon is one of the largest parks in the United States and includes wonderful forests, glacier canyons, and steep rock formations. This mountainous terrain was once inhabited by the Monache Indians, but the 1849 Gold Rush put an end to their way of life. Lumberjacks and farmers arrived next and stripped much of the forest, wreaking havoc on the natural environment.

There are those who would still like to take advantage of the area's rich natural resources, and only the 1940 creation of Kings Canyon National Park allowed the Kings River area to be preserved.

At the southern end of Sequoia National Park is the Giant Forest, one of the largest redwood forests on the planet. The giant sequoia known as General Sherman—named in honor of William Tecumseh Sherman by naturalist James Wolverton—is a record-breaker in terms of volume at just under 275 feet (83.8 meters) tall.

On the east side of the park is Mount Whitney, the tallest mountain in the United States at 14,505 feet (4,421 meters). It was named for geologist Josiah Whitney; Charles Begole, A. H. Johnson, and John Lucas were the first to summit the mountain in 1873.

Pp. 52-53: The sequoia forest, the heart of the park, is home to numerous examples of *Sequoiadendron giganteum*, the largest trees in the world. At one time these trees grew all over the American Northwest, but climate change and shifts in geology have reduced the area where they can thrive, and they now are found only in southern Sierra Nevada. Sequoia National Park, California.

Above: A tunnel through a giant redwood. Sequoia National Park, California.

Right: The tree known as General Sherman. At 275 feet (83.8 meters) tall and 52,508 cubic feet (1,500 cubic meters) in volume, it is considered the largest living tree on the planet and is one of the most photographed sights in the park. Sequoia National Park, California.

Pp. 56-57: Interior of the trunk of a giant redwood. Sequoia National Park, California.

Pp. 58-59: Moro Rock is a rock formation in Sequoia National Park, located between Giant Forest and Crescent Meadow. A long staircase allows visitors to hike to the top to enjoy sweeping views of mountains as high as 13,100 feet (4,000 meters). Sequoia National Park, California.

GENERAL SHERMAN

ABOVE: THE OPEN LANDSCAPE OF KINGS CANYON NATIONAL PARK, CALIFORNIA.

RIGHT: HIGHWAY 180, KINGS CANYON SCENIC BYWAY, WINDS THROUGH A FOREST OF PINE, FIR, AND CEDAR TREES AND OFFERS VIEWS OF THE RIVER AND THE ROCKY PEAKS IN THE DISTANCE.

DEATH VALLEY NATIONAL PARK

Death Valley National Park, located partly in California and partly in Nevada, is characterized by extremes. Native Americans called this area Tomesah, meaning "the place where the ground burns," due to the climate; indeed, temperatures in this area can reach 140 degrees Fahrenheit (60 degrees Celsius).

This arid land holds many surprises: rolling mountains, evaporated lakes, and salt pans that shimmer with iridescent rainbows. In spring and fall, the more mild temperatures highlight the natural vitality of the park.

Badwater Basin, the lowest point in North America, could pass for a lunar landscape. Zabriskie Point in the mountains is 5,000 feet (1,500 meters) from the valley floor, and the ghost town of Rhyolite was once a thriving mining community.

Scotty's Castle is a lavish home that belonged to a gold prospector and was funded by tycoon Albert M. Johnson.

ABOVE: NOT FAR FROM HIGHWAY 190, ZABRISKIE POINT OFFERS A SPLENDID VIEW OF THE HILLS OF THE GOLDEN CANYON. THIS AREA IS PART OF FURNACE CREEK, ALSO KNOWN AS THE BADLANDS DUE TO ITS EXTREMELY DRY AND SALINE SOIL. DEATH VALLEY NATIONAL PARK, CALIFORNIA.

Pp. 64-65: Scotty's Castle, in the northern part of the park, is one of Death Valley's most famous attractions. The Spanish-style villa has twenty-five rooms. Chicago billionaire Albert M. Johnson had it built in 1922, and it was then occupied by eccentric former prospector Walter Scott. The lavish interior reflects the opulence that preceded the Great Depression. Death Valley National Park, California.

Pp. 66-67: Sunsets are spectacular over Badwater Basin, the lowest point in the United States at 282 feet (86 meters) below sea level. The basin has a small amount of water with such high salt content that it is undrinkable—hence the name. The land here is often completely dry, and frosts and thaws, as well as evaporation, create the signature hexagonal formations on the ground. Death Valley National Park, California.

Opposite: Death Valley was once inaccessible to miners and explorers, but today cars can drive through this evocative landscape on extensive paved roads. Death Valley National Park, California.

JOSHUA TREE NATIONAL PARK

Joshua Tree National Park in southeast California was created in 1994 to protect the California desert and the Joshua tree, which is a species in the yucca family. Mormon settlers thought the trees resembled the prophet Joshua, who was said to pray with his hands reaching skyward toward God. Joshua trees can grow thirty feet (nine meters) high and live for thousands of years. They are the signature of this 1,235-square-mile (3,199-square-kilometer) park, which also features gray and pink rock formations, oases, and now-defunct mines. The park is home to some rare species of animals that have adapted to the severe habitat: the kangaroo rat has learned to extract food and water from seeds, while local jackrabbits have developed different fur colors to camouflage themselves and evade their predators, which include coyotes, eagles, and bobcats.

The park actually is made up of two different deserts with different ecosystems due to their disparate altitudes: the higher Mojave Desert and the lower Colorado Desert, part of the Sonora Desert. The San Bernardino Mountains run across the southwest border of the park.

The park's rock formations originated hundreds of millions of years ago when the magma below the Earth's surface cooled. The rock that formed then was eroded and shaped by underground streams that gave it the softer lines we see today. Later, water

OPPOSITE: THE MOJAVE DESERT JOSHUA TREE IS THE LARGEST YUCCA TREE. IT CAN GROW TO ABOUT THIRTY FEET (NINE METERS) IN HEIGHT AND LIVES AN AVERAGE OF 500 YEARS. THE NUMBER OF BRANCHES INDICATES A TREE'S AGE. JOSHUA TREE NATIONAL PARK, CALIFORNIA.

washed away the topsoil, further exposing boulders. Such rock formations are called monadnocks or inselbergs.

Many tried to tame this land, but only farmer and miner Bill Keys can be said to have truly succeeded. He and his family built the Desert Queen Ranch here and lived on the land for many years. The ranch and its garden and orchards—as well as some of the original farming equipment—can be seen today. Keys also built Barker Dam to contain rainwater and providing drinking water to his livestock and for use in the Desert Queen Mine.

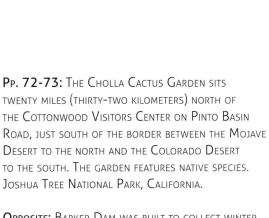

PP. 72-73: THE CHOLLA CACTUS GARDEN SITS TWENTY MILES (THIRTY-TWO KILOMETERS) NORTH OF THE COTTONWOOD VISITORS CENTER ON PINTO BASIN ROAD, JUST SOUTH OF THE BORDER BETWEEN THE MOJAVE DESERT TO THE NORTH AND THE COLORADO DESERT TO THE SOUTH. THE GARDEN FEATURES NATIVE SPECIES. JOSHUA TREE NATIONAL PARK, CALIFORNIA.

OPPOSITE: BARKER DAM WAS BUILT TO COLLECT WINTER RAINWATER THAT COULD THEN BE USED TO PROVIDE WATER FOR LIVESTOCK AND THE DESERT QUEEN MINE. MORE THAN A CENTURY AFTER ITS CREATION, THE SYSTEM STILL WORKS. JOSHUA TREE NATIONAL PARK, CALIFORNIA.

SOUTHWEST AND ROCKY MOUNTAINS

The Rocky Mountains run like a spine down North America, from British Columbia in Canada to New Mexico in the United States. This mountain range is justly famous for its environmental treasures, and the national parks in this area are among the most popular tourist destinations in the country.

These mountains formed about one hundred million years ago. They were a major challenge to early explorers and settlers. Today their evergreen forests, wide rivers, meadows full of brilliantly colored wildflowers, and mountainous tundra remain largely untouched, despite the accommodations made for the many tourists who visit the area. This wilderness is populated by large animals, including bears, elk, deer, buffalo, and antelopes.

Yet the environment, while precious, is only one part of what has been preserved here: this area offers the opportunity to learn about ancient traditions and study anthropological remains. Mesa Verde National Park preserves Anasazi cliff dwellings; Navajo still live amid the large stone towers in Monument Valley. The Grand Canyon can be viewed from above, but visitors can also follow the Colorado River and walk into the canyon itself. From this vantage point, the city of Las Vegas in Clark County looks like a far-off mirage in an otherwise empty desert.

YELLOWSTONE NATIONAL PARK

Yellowstone National Park encompasses a large area that straddles Wyoming, Montana, and Idaho. Founded in 1872, it was not only the first national park in the United States, but the first in the world.

The park is known for its many geological features: fumaroles, geysers, hot springs, and bubbling mud baths abound in the area. In most places, the Earth's crust is at least thirty miles (fifty kilometers) thick, but here it is one tenth that thickness, so water easily penetrates and comes into contact with the magma below. The water is then heated to high temperatures and spurts upward through the soil.

As a result, the land in this park is extremely active and is constantly changing. The geysers adhere to no set schedule, so their displays can come as a surprise and change the views dramatically in an instant. There are close to 300 geysers in Yellowstone; visitors are almost always treated to an amazing show as they walk the park's paths and walkways.

There is, however, one geyser that erupts like clockwork: Old Faithful. Every ninety minutes, it shoots out jets of water on average 145 feet (44 meters) into the air. Norris Geyser Basin sees intense volcanic activity. This area has hundreds of thermal baths, mud baths, and geysers, including Steamboat Geyser, which rises 300 feet (100 meters) into the air and the warm-water Firehole River with its many geyser basins.

This park has more than 1,240 miles (2,000 kilometers) in trails. They lead to popular sites such as Grand Prismatic Spring, famous for its rainbow-colored water. By car, horse, or on foot visitors can travel to other less crowded areas, which retain the feel of open space they must have offered early explorers.

Aside from the many interesting thermal

LEFT: THE COLORADO RIVER RUNS THROUGH THE EVER-IMPRESSIVE GRAND CANYON. GRAND CANYON NATIONAL PARK.

phenomena, the park is full of natural beauty: evergreen forests, canyons, waterfalls, and lakes. It is home to about sixty different types of mammals, 300 different species of birds, and eighteen different species of marine life.

Mammoth and Geyser Country are the most popular areas, and these two areas alone would form a park that would draw visitors, but there's more: Yellowstone Lake in Lake Country is one of the largest mountain lakes in the world with its 136-square-mile (350-square-kilometer) basin.

In the northeast of the park, named Roosevelt Country, buffalo and elk graze along the Bannock Trail.

And the Yellowstone River rushes through the untamed heart of the park, Canyon Country. The river's water runs between yellow and red rock face.

Close to 900 grizzly bears live in this park. Their hunched backs and gray-streaked fur are unmistakable. In 1995, wolves were reintroduced to this area after seventy years, as it was recognized that they are part of the delicately balanced ecosystem that keeps animal populations, bodies of water, and plant life in check.

P. 77: Multicolored Grand Prismatic Spring is the largest hot spring in the United States. Its kaleidoscopic colors range from cool blue to bright red due to bacteria in the water. Yellowstone National Park, Wyoming.

Opposite: The magnificent travertine hills of Mammoth Hot Springs. Because the water has a high calcium content, the hot springs are constantly shifting. As a result, trees are swallowed up by the more recent travertine deposits, while vegetation grows freely around the springs. Yellowstone National Park, Wyoming.

OPPOSITE: OLD FAITHFUL IS ONE OF THE WORLD'S MOST FAMOUS GEYSERS. THE WASHBURN-LANGFORD-DOANE EXPEDITION NAMED THE GEYSER AFTER OBSERVING ITS REGULAR ERUPTIONS, WHICH SHOOT BOILING WATER AN AVERAGE OF 145 FEET (44 METERS) INTO THE AIR. YELLOWSTONE NATIONAL PARK, WYOMING.

PP. 82-83: ABYSS POOL HOT SPRING IN WEST THUMB GEYSER BASIN. THE CLEAR QUALITY OF ITS BOILING WATER MAKES THE BASIN SEEM DEEPER THAN IT IS—FIFTY-THREE FEET (SIXTEEN METERS). IT ERUPTS ONLY OCCASIONALLY, SENDING WATER THIRTY FEET (NINE METERS) INTO THE AIR. YELLOWSTONE NATIONAL PARK, WYOMING.

PP. 84-85: BUFFALO GRAZE ON THE BANKS OF FIREHOLE RIVER. THIS PARK IS HOME TO SEVERAL DIFFERENT TYPES OF LARGE MAMMALS. STRICT REGULATIONS SAFEGUARD THEM AND REQUIRE TOURISTS TO STAY AT LEAST 100 YARDS (NINETY-ONE METERS) FROM BEARS AND TWENTY-FIVE YARDS (TWENTY-THREE METERS) FROM OTHER ANIMALS. YELLOWSTONE NATIONAL PARK, WYOMING.

PP. 86-87: THE SPECTACULAR UPPER YELLOWSTONE FALLS, WHERE THE YELLOWSTONE RIVER VEERS FROM ITS SOUTHEAST COURSE AND RUNS FOR TWENTY MILES (THIRTY-TWO KILOMETERS) THROUGH A CANYON. YELLOWSTONE NATIONAL PARK, WYOMING.

GRAND TETON NATIONAL PARK

Grand Teton National Park in Wyoming is 485,000 square miles (1,254 square kilometers) and includes the Teton Range, the most recently formed mountains in the Rockies, some of the most beautiful mountains in the world.

French-Canadians who traversed the area for the Northwest Company, a fur and leather trading company in business from 1779 to 1821, gave the mountain range its name (which means "large breasts").

The many miles of trails in the park run alongside lakes and glaciers. The wildlife in the park includes elks, buffalo, and bears. Jackson Hole in the valley of the Snake River between the Gros Ventre Range and the Grand Teton Range offers a perfect spot for taking in this sheer rock face, which climbs to 13,000 feet (4,000 meters).

The park was created in 1929 and later expanded when wealthy businessman John D. Rockefeller, Jr. donated additional land. Along with Yellowstone National Park, Grand Teton National Park is part of the Greater Yellowstone Ecosystem, one of the largest intact ecosystems in North America and a place where many buffalo and grizzly bears have been preserved.

OPPOSITE: A LONE FISHER ON THE SNAKE RIVER. GRAND TETON NATIONAL PARK, WYOMING.

PP. 90-91: T. A. MOULTON BARN AT THE FOOT OF THE TETON RANGE WAS THE HOME OF THOMAS ALMA MOULTON AND HIS SON FROM ABOUT 1912 TO 1945. THE MUCH-PHOTOGRAPHED BARN HAS BECOME A SYMBOL OF JACKSON HOLE. GRAND TETON NATIONAL PARK, WYOMING.

Pp. 92-93: Maple trees wearing their fall colors in Grand Teton National Park, Wyoming.

Opposite: Jenny Lake, formed by glaciers, is a star attraction in Grand Teton National Park. Several different footpaths lead to its shores, and boating is permitted on the lake itself as well. Grand Teton National Park, Wyoming.

GLACIER
NATIONAL PARK

Glacier National Park in the northern Rocky Mountains is located in northern Montana along the Continental Divide. The park is more than one million acres (4,000 square kilometers) and includes twenty-seven small glaciers.

The park land goes from 3,280 feet to close to 10,000 feet (1,000 to 3,000 meters) above sea level, and the landscape is varied and encompasses two different mountain ranges, more than 130 lakes, waterfalls, limestone

rock walls, grassy meadows, and alpine tundra.

In the summer the meadows are bursting with color as irises, gentians, heather, and bear grass flower.

Naturalist John Muir decreed that spending at least one month here served as a cure for stress and worry. In *Our National Parks* (1901), he wrote, "Get off the track at Belton Station, and in a few minutes you will find yourself in the midst of what you are sure to say is the best care-killing scenery on the continent."

The animal life in the park and the large network of paths here are also a draw, and the park is the center of a large protected area. National forests sit to the south and the west of the park, while its north side borders Waterton Lakes National Park in Canada.

PP. 96-97: LAKE MCDONALD, THE LARGEST BODY
OF WATER IN THE PARK, REFLECTS ITS SURROUNDINGS.
GLACIER NATIONAL PARK, MONTANA.

PP. 98-99: TURQUOISE WATER POOLS AT THE BASE OF
GRINNELL GLACIER, WHICH HAS SHRUNK SIGNIFICANTLY.
IT WAS NAMED FOR EXPLORER GEORGE BIRD GRINNELL,
A STRONG SUPPORTER OF PRESERVATION EFFORTS IN THE
AREA. GLACIER NATIONAL PARK, MONTANA.

OPPOSITE: GOING-TO-THE-SUN ROAD RUNS FOR ABOUT
FIFTY MILES (EIGHTY KILOMETERS) THROUGH THE PARK AND
CROSSES THE CONTINENTAL DIVIDE AT ITS HIGHEST POINT.
A SERIES OF LOOKOUT POINTS OFFER AMAZING VIEWS.
GLACIER NATIONAL PARK, MONTANA.

BADLANDS
NATIONAL PARK

Badlands National Park is the largest park in South Dakota and is known for its meadows and its dramatic rock formations: buttes, pinnacles, and stratified sandstone spires combine in a beautiful labyrinth. The park is more than 242,000 acres (98,000 hectares). In addition to its interesting geological features and plant life, the park is home to bison, bighorn sheep, deer, pronghorn, prairie dogs, and black-footed ferrets that share space with birds, reptiles, and butterflies.

Sioux Indians referred to this area as *mako sica*, or "land bad." Indeed,

this was inhospitable terrain, both because it was so rugged and difficult to travel and because there was little water available. This is a park that seems to change at a fast clip: the soil erodes at the incredible speed of about a half-inch (one centimeter) per year. Because of the shifting soil, many fossils have been found here.

Before Badlands was protected—it became a national monument in 1929 and a national park in 1978—anyone who wished to do so could dig for fossils in the area.

The park's unusual rock formations date to the late Cretaceous Period, Eocene Epoch, and Oligocene Epoch and derive from sediment left behind by a body of water that once covered the prairie. Later, streams and flood plains added to the deposits.

While the era when most of this material was deposited ended 28,000 years ago, significant erosion of the Badlands began only about a half-million years ago. This phenomenon is still sculpting the area today; it is believe that at some point the Badlands will be completely eroded.

The fossils in the park are not dinosaur fossils, but instead are from marine species and extinct mammals, including the precursors to modern rhinoceroses, horses, pigs, and cats. Bird, reptile, and invertebrate fossils have also been found here.

This is an important place for Native Americans, and Badlands National Park established a partnership with the Oglala Sioux in 1976. The arrangement calls for sharing land, namely the area known as the South Unit, and dividing up proceeds from entry fees. The tribe receives half of the proceeds for resource management and various projects.

Overhead the park offers excellent visibility of the stars and galaxies, as well as star clusters, nebulae, planets, and the moon. The view of the Milky Way from the park is exceptionally clear.

Pp. 102-103: When the sun goes down, Badlands National Park shows its best side. Shadows highlight the many crevasses and peaks, and the white, gray, brown, red, and purple stripes on the rock formations stand out. Badlands National Park, South Dakota.

Pp. 104-105: Badlands Loop State Scenic Byway (Route 240) is a two-lane road that runs through the park for thirty miles (forty-eight kilometers). It follows the northern side of Badlands Walls and offers breathtaking views of the sharp drops of the rock formations. Badlands National Park, South Dakota.

Opposite: Rock formations were created by mud deposits from the nearby Black Hills, then shaped by the wind and sun. Badlands National Park, South Dakota.

ROCKY MOUNTAIN NATIONAL PARK

Rocky Mountain National Park in northern Colorado offers some of the most beautiful views in the entire country. Created in 1915, the park is 265,460 acres (1,075 square kilometers) and contains not only a vast array of fauna and flora, but 114 peaks above 10,000 feet (3,000 meters). The tallest of these is Longs Peak, named for Stephen Harriman Long, who led an expedition through this area in 1820. Longs Peak is 14,259 feet (4,346 meters) high.

The Continental Divide (which determines whether rivers in the United States will run into the Atlantic Ocean or the Pacific Ocean) cuts through the park. The portion of the park on the western side of the Continental Divide tends to be drier with snowy peaks, while the eastern side has a more humid climate, more green plant life, and areas of dense forest.

Trail Ridge Road, which is forty-eight miles (almost eighty kilometers) long runs through the park and reaches an elevation of 12,1835 feet (3,713 meters). The road opens up to spectacular views of lakes and frozen tundra, and the ample wildlife in the park, including elk, moose, black bears, and bighorn sheep, can be seen from it.

ABOVE: VIEW OF THE ROCK CUT MOUNTAINS FROM TRAIL RIDGE ROAD, ONE OF THE MOST SCENIC ROUTES IN NORTH AMERICA AND THE MAIN ROAD THROUGH THE PARK. THE ROAD IS OPEN FROM MAY THROUGH OCTOBER AND OFFERS GORGEOUS VIEWS. ROCKY MOUNTAIN NATIONAL PARK, COLORADO.

RIGHT: LONGS PEAK, IN THE SOUTHEASTERN PART OF THE PARK, LOOMS ABOVE THE SURROUNDING AREA AT AN ALTITUDE OF 14,259 FEET (4,346 METERS). ROCKY MOUNTAIN NATIONAL PARK, COLORADO.

PP. 110-111: LUMPY RIDGE, IN THE NORTHEAST OF THE PARK, CONSISTS OF A SERIES OF GRANITE WALLS ERODED BY WATER AND ICE—A POPULAR DESTINATION FOR ROCK CLIMBERS FROM ALL OVER THE WORLD. ROCKY MOUNTAIN NATIONAL PARK, COLORADO.

Pp. 112-113: Bear Lake sits at high altitude. Rocky Mountain National Park, Colorado.

Opposite: The Rocky Mountains run north-south and are home to an extremely wide variety of animals. The large mammals in the mountainous areas of Rocky Mountain National Park include many elk.

ARCHES NATIONAL PARK

Arches National Park was created in 1971. It counts nearly 120 square miles (310 square kilometers) in eastern Utah and has the largest number of natural stone arches of any place on the planet.

The Colorado River marks the southern border of the park, which is equal parts untamed wilderness and carefully tended garden. The park has about 1,700 stone arches, as well as other giant rock formations: steeples, pinnacles, and hanging rocks.

These formations were largely created by salt. Salt deposits formed in the subsoil approximately 300 million years ago, when the area was covered by shallow but vast seas that then evaporated when the climate became drier. For example, Paradox Basin has layers of salt hundreds of yards deep. During the Jurassic period, flood detritus and sand were carried by the wind and landed here, where they settled on top of salt to create a large desert. This material slowly solidified and took on a reddish pink hue due to infiltration of iron oxide. The rocks exerted pressure on the salt and the layer of salt began to move, sliding back and forth and causing the rock on top to move as well. These movements in turn caused vertical fractures; erosion then took over and formed pinnacles and arches. New arches are still being shaped today, and occasionally an old arch crumbles. In other words, erosion is ongoing, and it is still changing the scenery that makes Arches National Park a truly unique treasure.

OPPOSITE: DELICATE ARCH IS A FAVORITE IN THE PARK AND A SYMBOL OF UTAH; IT IS EVEN DEPICTED ON THE STATE'S LICENSE PLATES. THE ARCH IS LOCATED IN A NATURAL AMPHITHEATER THAT OFFERS VIEWS OF THE SURROUNDING VALLEY AND THE LA SAL MOUNTAINS. ARCHES NATIONAL PARK, UTAH.

Pp. 118-119: Fiery Furnace is a natural maze with narrow paths and canyons carved in the rock. Arches National Park, Utah.

Above: At nearly 300 feet (ninety-one meters) Landscape Arch is considered the longest natural arch in the world. Arches National Park, Utah.

Right: Sand Dune Arch is not known for its size or shape, but for the landscape that surrounds it, which is undeniably evocative. A narrow path through the rocks leads to the arch, located in an area with particularly fine sand. Arches National Park, Utah.

LEFT: BALANCED ROCK, IN THE PARK'S WINDOWS SECTION, IS A ROCKY STEEPLE WITH A LARGE ROCK BALANCED ATOP IT THAT SEEMS TO DEFY GRAVITY. IT CAN BE SPOTTED FROM THE DISTANCE, EVEN AS FAR AWAY AS THE MAIN ROAD. ARCHES NATIONAL PARK, UTAH.

ABOVE: ONE OF MANY FASCINATING SIGHTS IN THE PARK'S WINDOWS SECTION: TURRET ARCH FRAMED BY THE NORTH WINDOW. ARCHES NATIONAL PARK, UTAH.

PP. 124-125: PARK AVENUE IS A SHORT PATH LINED WITH TALL, VERTICAL-WALLED ROCK FORMATIONS THAT RESEMBLE SKYSCRAPERS. ARCHES NATIONAL PARK, UTAH.

GRAND CANYON NATIONAL PARK

At more than 1,200,000 acres (more than 4,900 square kilometers), Grand Canyon National Park contains all of the gigantic canyon for which it is named, ranging from the point where the Paria River merges with the Colorado River near Lees Ferry all the way to Lake Mead.

This area became a national monument in 1908 and was declared a national park in 1919. The Grand Canyon is one of the Seven Wonders of the World and an emblem of the United States, and as a result this is one of the country's best known national parks.

The park is loosely divided into the South Rim, which attracts most of the tourists who visit, and the North Rim, which sits at a higher altitude and is a little more untamed. Additionally, the Havasupai Indian Reservation is located west of the South Rim, and the Toroweap Valley, on the other side of the canyon, borders the Lake Mead National Recreation Area. These two areas are the most isolated parts of the park and are not very accessible to tourists.

The North Rim and the South Rim face each other and at a glance appear close to each other, but they are separated by that enormous gorge, which at its widest points is eighteen miles (thirty kilometers) across. In order to travel from one area to the other, visitors need to travel a lengthy road by car, passing through Marble Canyon. Indeed, the North Rim and the South Rim are almost like separate worlds: they have different plant life, different types of rocks, and even different animals. The Kaibab squirrels that live in the South Rim, for example, are quite different from the Kanab squirrels in the North Rim, and it is believed that these two species have never encountered each other.

The Grand Canyon is the result of a fascinating geological phenomenon. In order to understand how it was created, you need to look back at the geological history of this part of the world.

Millions of years ago, the oceans covered Arizona. Study of the top layers of soil demonstrates that this was the case.

The Grand Canyon is a wide fracture in a relatively flat area of land that runs for miles. This large chasm was created by the Colorado River six million years ago. Here and there in the canyon there are stone steeples that pop up as if a divine hand had placed them in those particular locations.

The wind is harsh here and buffets the sandstone and limestone rock face, and it has eroded them over the years. Rainwater has sculpted the rock here, as has the water from melting snow, albeit more gently. The water infiltrated deep into the rock through cracks and when it froze it eroded even more rock. In this way the canyon "expanded" over the years. The results are nothing short of spectacular. Vertical rock face formed where the rock was harder; slanted rock face marks the spots where the rock was softer.

The canyon's size is certainly striking, but its colors are no less fascinating. There is an endless play of light and shadow on the rock, and the various hues witnessed seem to shimmer. The Grand Canyon's beauty is simply stunning.

Opposite: Powell Point, on the South Rim, provides a view of the canyon, which is more than a mile deep. In the 1800s, explorer John Wesley Powell called it "the most sublime spectacle in nature." The Colorado River runs through the canyon. Grand Canyon National Park, Arizona.

Pp. 128-129: Mather Point on the South Rim of Grand Canyon. Mather Point is one of the first overlooks visitors encounter when entering the park at the south entrance, and many are struck breathless by their initial view of the vastness of this landscape, stretching from Bright Angel Trail to South Kaibab Trail. The spot is named for Stephen Mather, the first national parks director and a major supporter, who both boosted the park's profile and helped to promote tourism to the area. Grand Canyon National Park, Arizona.

Pp. 130-131: View of the Grand Canyon from Moran Point on the South Rim. Moran Point was named for artist Peter Moran, who visited the South Rim with explorer Captain John Bourke in 1882. Various rock formations and the Colorado River can be viewed from this spot. Moran Point is accessed via Desert View Drive, a twenty-five-mile (forty-kilometer) road that connects Grand Canyon Village to the Watchtower, a stone tower designed by architect Mary Colter and built in 1932. Grand Canyon National Park, Arizona.

Opposite: The Colorado River, Aha Kwahwat in Mojave, rushes through the Grand Canyon. The 1,450-mile (2,300-kilometer) river begins at La Poudre Pass in Rocky Mountain National Park and crosses the west side of the Rocky Mountains, emptying into the Gulf of California. The Natural Resources Defense Council reports that climate change poses a serious threat to the river, as rising temperatures have caused snow to melt, as well as raising the temperature along the riverbed and reducing the volume of water. Grand Canyon National Park, Arizona.

Pp. 134-135: Sunset over the Grand Canyon, seen from the North Rim. Only about ten percent of visitors to the park travel to the north side of the canyon, which has remained less developed and is also a little harder to access and at a higher altitude. The two sides of the canyon have eroded in disparate ways, so the rock formations known as "temples" are more visible on this side. Grand Canyon National Park, Arizona.

MESA VERDE
NATIONAL PARK

Mesa Verde National Park in Colorado centers around a wooded mesa that looms over Montezuma Valley and contains archeological sites composed of many cliff-dwellings that were dug into the canyon rock.

Mesa Verde, or "green table," is the name the Spanish gave to the area in the 1800s; the Pueblo ruins would not be discovered until the end of that century. During the time of the Roman Empire in Europe, in the early Middle Ages, inhabitants settled in this area more than 8,000 feet (2,500 meters) above sea level.

Among the more interesting sites here is Cliff Palace, which has 150 rooms and is the largest village on the cliffs. It was built around 1200 and abandoned in 1275.

Mesa Verde National Park counts nearly 500 archeological sites. The area was abandoned in the early fourteenth century for reasons that remain unclear. When President Theodore Roosevelt established a national park here in 1906, he aimed not only to preserve natural resources, but also to maintain the archeological treasure found here.

ABOVE: CLIFF-DWELLINGS WERE PREHISTORIC RESIDENCES BUILT IN THE NATURAL CAVES OF THE CANYON. THE PUEBLO PEOPLE LIVED, WORKED, AND PERFORMED RELIGIOUS RITUALS HERE. FOR REASONS THAT REMAIN UNCLEAR, THE AREA WAS ABANDONED AROUND 1300. IT BECAME A NATIONAL PARK IN 1906. MESA VERDE NATIONAL PARK, COLORADO.

RIGHT: BALCONY HOUSE WAS AN AVERAGE-SIZED CLIFF-DWELLING WITH APPROXIMATELY FORTY ROOMS. IT CAN BE SEEN FROM CLIFF PALACE LOOP. S. E. OSBORNE WAS THE FIRST TO EXPLORE THIS SITE IN 1884. TODAY VISITORS CLIMB A LADDER AND THEN PASS THROUGH A TUNNEL IN ORDER TO VISIT IT. MESA VERDE NATIONAL PARK, COLORADO.

Left: Long House on Wetherill Mesa in the western part of the park. The site was studied from 1959 to 1961 as part of the Wetherill Mesa Archeological Project and opened to the public in 1973. This area preserves some of the most characteristic Pueblo cliff dwellings. It is believed to have been a communal structure of about 150 rooms on three floors. Mesa Verde National Park, Colorado.

Above: View of Montezuma Valley from the Geologic Overlook. The San Juan Mountains stand in the background. Mesa Verde National Park, Colorado.

BRYCE CANYON NATIONAL PARK

Bryce Canyon National Park was formed in 1928. This Utah park has some of the world's most intriguing and colorful rock formations, a kaleidoscope of reds, oranges, and yellows. At least sixty different colors have been identified. The area is know for hoodoos, pinnacles formed by wind, snow, and rain erosion that heavily impacts the calcareous rock. Paiute natives believed that hoodoos were their ancestors turned to stone, and they called the canyon *ankakuwassawets*, meaning "faces painted red."

Despite the name of the park, Bryce Canyon is not actually a canyon. It is instead a group of calcareous rock formations that have eroded along the eastern side. The most famous of these is the Bryce Amphitheater, a standout in the park. Other rock formations are fins, slot canyons, bridges, and arches. All show the results of a long legacy of sedimentation and erosion.

The park was named for pioneer Ebenezer Bryce. It is 35,835 acres (145 square kilometers) and sits at 8,000 to 9,000 feet (2,400 to 2,700 meters) above sea level. Mormons settled in this area beginning in 1850, and it was named a national monument in 1924.

OPPOSITE: BRIGHT WHITE SNOW CONTRASTS WITH THE RED ROCKS IN WINTER. BRYCE CANYON NATIONAL PARK, UTAH.

Pp. 142-143: The altitude in Bryce Canyon varies by about 1,000 feet (300 meters) to create three separate climactic zones: juniper and pine forest, Ponderosa pine forest, and fir forest. Bryce Canyon National Park, Utah.

Pp. 144-145: Spectacular rock formations. Bryce Canyon National Park, Utah.

Opposite: Bryce Point is a popular spot and offers a sweeping view of the amphitheater below. At dawn and dusk warm light slants in to create a fascinating play of light and shadows, and the hoodoos almost look as though they are on fire. The park was named for Ebenezer Bryce, by all accounts a skilled tradesman, who settled in the area in 1875. Bryce Canyon National Park, Utah.

ZION NATIONAL PARK

President Theodore Roosevelt declared Zion in Utah a protected area in 1909, but it would only become a national park a decade later, in 1919.

At nearly 230 square miles (593 square kilometers), Zion National Park has an altitude that varies from 3,666 feet (1,128 meters) at its lowest point, on the Coal Pits Wash bed, to 8,726 feet (2,660 meters) at its highest point on Horse Ranch Mountain.

The heart of this park is Zion Canyon, which was carved here by the Virgin River and then expanded further by wind, rain, and ice. The canyon walls are 2,000 feet (600 meters) high in places, and its most notable feature is the jagged outline of the rocks and their color, which ranges

from red to white. Various types of animals graze on the plants that grow along the river bed.

This canyon is strikingly large and picturesque. The rock formations look like sculptures by some prehistoric artist, while the lush vegetation—wildflowers, black poplar, willows, and oak trees—make it clear why the Mormon pioneers who arrived here in the mid-nineteenth century thought they had found paradise.

The park's name was adopted officially in 1918 and was given to it by one of the early Mormon settlers who arrived in 1863, Isaac Behunin, who believed he had stumbled upon the Zion described by the prophet Isaiah in the bible. There are other biblical names in the park as well,

including the Watchman, the Three Patriarchs, and the Temples and Towers of the Virgin, all named by a Methodist minister who visited the area in 1916.

Frequent flooding has stymied development in this area, leaving it intact. It still feels like a secret and special place.

Pp. 148-149: ZION CANYON WAS CARVED FIRST BY
THE VIRGIN RIVER, THEN BY WIND, RAIN, AND ICE. BLACK
POPLARS, WILLOWS, OAKS, AND NUMEROUS FLOWERS GROW
ON THE RIVER'S BANKS, AND THE CANYON WALLS EXHIBIT A
RANGE OF HUES FROM DEEP RED TO WHITE. ZION NATIONAL
PARK, UTAH.

ABOVE: OBSERVATION POINT, 6,500 FEET (1,980
METERS) HIGH OFFERS SENSATIONAL VIEWS OF THE VALLEY
AND ROCK FORMATIONS ALONG THE VIRGIN RIVER. THE
MOUNTAINS PROVIDE AN EVOCATIVE BACKDROP. ZION

NATIONAL PARK, UTAH.

RIGHT: THE SUBWAY, ALSO KNOWN AS LEFT FORK OF
NORTH CREEK, IS A SLOT CANYON THAT RESEMBLES A TUNNEL
DUG THROUGH THE ROCK. ZION NATIONAL PARK, UTAH.

Pp. 152-153: THE ROCKS IN ZION CANYON ARE CRUMBLY,
WHICH ACCOUNTS FOR THE NUMEROUS CREVASSES AND
BRIDGES IN THE U-SHAPED CANYON. THE RED AND PINK
COLORS IN THE ROCK ARE DUE TO IRON IN THE WATER. ZION
NATIONAL PARK, UTAH

PETRIFIED FOREST NATIONAL PARK

Nearly 150 square miles (370 square kilometers) of arid desert with low-lying bushes and shrubs exists in northeastern Arizona. Pastel-colored hills, basins, and plains combine to create a dreamlike scene.

Though at first glance Petrified Forest National Park seems completely empty, it actually contains some precious treasures: the largest deposit of petrified wood in the world and the archeological remains and graffiti of ancient peoples who lived here for almost 8,000 years.

The park sits on both sides of Interstate 40. The entrance on the north side offers the best views of the Painted Desert. Millions of years ago, conifers up to 200 feet (sixty meters) tall grew in this valley, which was green and swampy at the time. After the trees fell, they were covered in mud and mineral-rich volcanic ash that kept them from giving off oxygen and slowed decomposition. Fragments of silica gradually infiltrated the tree trunks, creating colorful quartz crystals, jasper, and amethyst.

The Anasazi were attracted to these multicolored rocks and used the petrified wood to create weapons and other objects. The forest remained intact for centuries, until tourism and trade began to develop in the nineteenth century, putting this area at risk. The earliest local movements to protect the region were begun in 1895, and in 1906 the Petrified Forest National Monument was created; it became a national park officially in 1962.

Pp. 154-155: This stone forest is one of Arizona's most unusual attractions. The Painted Desert runs the length of the park and features strips of colored sand and rocks that shimmer in the sunlight.

Pp. 156-157: The hills, canyons, and mesas in the Painted Desert change color constantly and look brighter during summer storms. Colorful Chinle formation rock is made of sand, clay, and lime and

is particularly brittle, making it subject to erosion. Petrified Forest National Park, Arizona..

Above and right: The fossilized trunks of the Petrified Forest can be seen in Jasper Forest and Crystal Forest. They consist of towering conifers that grew in the area about 225 million years ago. When the trees fell, rivers carried them to a swamp. Then silicon dioxide in the water transformed the wood with colorful quartz crystals that

reproduced the shape of the trees. The Anasazi Indians were fascinated by this fossilized wood and used it to create all kinds of objects. Petrified Forest National Park, Arizona.

VOYAGEURS NATIONAL PARK

Located in Minnesota near the Canadian border, Voyageurs National Park was created in 1975. The name refers to French-Canadian fur traders, the first Europeans in the area. The park is known for its many bodies of water: lakes, springs, swamps, and ponds populated by beavers and dotted with small islands that attract packs of wolves.

The damp Rainy Lake area, west of the Superior National Forest, was once accessed via the Voyageur's Highway, a network of lakes, streams, and other crossings used by both Natives and fur traders who traveled from the Ontario and Minnesota woods as far as Montreal, crossing the Great Lakes.

The park not only has large bodies of water, but it is also a major spot for preservation of wolves, especially gray wolves. The Dakota Indians called this land *minisota*, which means "land of sky-blue water." Minnesota today is still known for its pristine forests and waters.

OPPOSITE: VIEW OF LAKE KABETOGAMA. THE BEST WAY TO TOUR THE PARK IS TO TRAVEL ITS NETWORK OF LAKES, STREAMS, AND OTHER WATERWAYS BY BOAT OR CANOE, JUST AS NATIVE AMERICANS AND FUR TRADERS ONCE DID. KABETOGAMA PENINSULA HAS NO ROADS. VOYAGEURS NATIONAL PARK, MINNESOTA.

EAST COAST

When the first Europeans reached the East Coast of the United States, they found a difficult and sometimes unpredictable climate. As they settled on hills with dense forests, they realized that in order to survive they would need to develop a strong spirit of independence and the ability to adapt. Today the East Coast still reflects that grit and determination. The state motto of New Hampshire, "Live free or die," reflects the attitude of those early colonists and could easily be the motto of the entire region.

The Atlantic seaboard is also the most densely populated area of the United States. Boston, New York, Philadelphia, and Washington are all located here. From northern New England down the length of the coastline, though, large cities are balanced by wild and peaceful rural areas. Some of the country's loveliest national parks are surprisingly close to its large metropolitan areas.

ACADIA NATIONAL PARK

Even before Mount Desert Island, off the southeast coast of Maine, was named a national monument in 1916 and then became the core of this national park in 1929, it was a popular destination for naturalists and tourists. It has beautiful mountains and lakes and a characteristic coastline.

On the island a large natural fjord shaped like a finger creates a barrier between quiet Southwest Harbour and the more animated Northeast Harbour.

Though Acadia National Park (which encompasses much of the island) is one of the smallest national parks in the country at seventy-four square miles (192 square kilometers), it contains many treasures, including a steep rocky coast, woods, mountains, fjords, and bays.

The land here still shows traces of the Ice Age, when weather phenomena sculpted the rock in unusual ways. Long valleys, lakes, rock formations, and bare mountaintops combine to create breathtaking beauty.

More than fifty species of mammals live in the park, and more than 300 species of animals such as deer, foxes, skunks, porcupines, beavers, muskrats, groundhogs, and sea eagles. Seals love to sun on the rocks on the shores of the smaller islands.

Many different bird species build their nests in this park, including terns, plovers, and numerous types of ducks and gulls.

P. 162: Abrams Falls are a popular attraction in the Great Smoky Mountains National Park. Though not impressively tall, they make a great deal of noise and their water flow is abundant. They were named for the chief of a nearby Cherokee village. Great Smoky Mountains National Park, Tennessee.

Opposite: Birch trees in the autumn light in Acadia National Park, Maine.

Farther in there are hawks, woodpeckers, and many small species of birds. Sometimes owls can be spotted. Turtles and non-poisonous snakes are also native to the area.

The park was created through the joint efforts of Maine residents and scions of wealthy families who had summer homes here and donated land to the effort. John D. Rockefeller Jr. was a major contributor. His most visible gift was the network of roads created in 1913. Rockefeller didn't cotton to the idea of allowing cars on the island, so he provided funds for fifty miles of gravel carriage roads.

P. 164: Cadillac Mountain (1,527 feet or 466 meters) is the highest elevation on the North Atlantic coast. Many visitors hike to the pink granite peak to watch the sun set over the Atlantic Ocean. Acadia National Park, Maine.

P. 165: Jordan Pond seen from the North Bubble. This small lake was formed by a glacier and is 150 feet (forty-six meters) deep at its deepest point. Canoes and kayaks are allowed on the lakes, but motorboats are not. The lake is close to Bar Harbour, Penobscot Mountain, and the two mountains known as "the Bubbles." Acadia National Park, Maine.

Opposite: The town of Bass Harbor sits on Maine's rocky coast, at the southern tip of Mount Desert Island. A picturesque 1858 lighthouse looks out over the water. Acadia National Park, Maine.

Pp. 168-169: Fall foliage displays its many colors. Acadia National Park, Maine.

CUYAHOGA VALLEY NATIONAL PARK

Cuyahoga Valley National Park in Ohio may reside only a short distance from the cities of Cleveland and Akron, but it is a world apart, completely separate from urban hustle and bustle.

The park is home to native plant and animal life, and the winding Cuyahoga River is lined with lush forests and rolling hills. The park also contains several working farms, where visitors can witness the methods used for centuries to farm this land.

The name of the Cuyahoga River comes from an Indian word meaning "winding river," and this river lives up to that moniker. It runs between two large cities.

ABOVE: VIBRANT HUES LIGHT UP THE PARK IN AUTUMN. CUYAHOGA VALLEY NATIONAL PARK, OHIO.

171

LEFT: BRANDYWINE FALLS ARE ONE OF THE MAIN ATTRACTIONS IN CUYAHOGA VALLEY NATIONAL PARK. THE FALLS WERE AN IMPORTANT ENERGY SOURCE FOR EUROPEAN COLONISTS. AN EARLY MILL BUILT IN 1814 LED TO INCREASING DEVELOPMENT IN THE VALLEY. THE FALLS CAN BE OBSERVED FROM A SERIES OF WOODEN STAIRCASES AND VIEWING PLATFORMS. CUYAHOGA VALLEY NATIONAL PARK, OHIO.

ABOVE: THE BUTTERMILK FALLS ARE SMALL BUT SCENIC AND CAN BE ACCESSED VIA A TRAIL OFF OF BOSTON MILLS ROAD. CUYAHOGA VALLEY NATIONAL PARK, OHIO.

ABOVE AND RIGHT: HALE FARM AND VILLAGE PRESERVES
TWO CENTURIES OF THE HISTORY OF THE FIRST SETTLERS IN
THE CUYAHOGA VALLEY. VISITORS TO THE MUSEUM, CREATED
IN 1958, CAN EXPERIENCE THE LIFE OF EARLY COLONISTS.
CUYAHOGA VALLEY NATIONAL PARK, OHIO.

PP. 176-177: A SMALL WATERFALL ON DEER LICK CREEK,
ONE OF THE PRETTIEST SPOTS IN THE STATE OF OHIO. CUYAHOGA
VALLEY NATIONAL PARK, OHIO.

SHENANDOAH NATIONAL PARK

Shenandoah National Park, located a short seventy-five miles (120 kilometers) from Washington, D.C., is a 200,000-acre (800-square-kilometer) oasis that residents of the surrounding cities enjoy greatly. Waterfalls, streams, woods, and spectacular views draw human visitors, but the park is also home to deer, black bears, and other animals native to the area. There are also a large number of aquatic insects that thrive in the damp, cold climate in these mountains.

The park includes the Blue Ridge Mountains in the southern Appalachians, bordered to the east by the Virginian Piedmont and to the west by the Shenandoah Valley. Its two largest mountains, Stony Man Mountain and Hawksbill Mountain, provide a range of altitudes, rock formations, and types of soil. In short, the habitat is widely varied.

The first European settlers here were farmers. When the park was created in the 1920s and 1930s, they moved out of the area. A few grave markers and the remains of some of their homes can still be seen today.

OPPOSITE: SHENANDOAH VALLEY IS PART OF THE GREAT APPALACHIAN VALLEY AND IS BORDERED BY THE BLUE RIDGE MOUNTAINS TO THE EAST AND THE RIDGE-AND-VALLEY APPALACHIANS AND THE ALLEGHENY MOUNTAINS TO THE WEST. SHENANDOAH IS A NATIVE WORD THAT MEANS "BEAUTIFUL DAUGHTER OF THE STARS." SHENANDOAH NATIONAL PARK, VIRGINIA.

PP. 180-181: THE SHENANDOAH MOUNTAINS CLOAKED IN AUTUMN FOG. SHENANDOAH NATIONAL PARK, VIRGINIA.

ABOVE: THE EASTERN TIGER SWALLOWTAIL BUTTERFLY IS ONE
OF THE MOST COMMON IN THE EASTERN UNITED STATES.
SHENANDOAH NATIONAL PARK, VIRGINIA.

RIGHT: A WHITE-TAILED DEER FAWN STANDS ON SPINDLY LEGS.
SHENANDOAH NATIONAL PARK, VIRGINIA.

182

GREAT SMOKY MOUNTAINS NATIONAL PARK

Chartered in 1934, this national park includes the Great Smoky Mountains (so named because of the smoky-looking fog that wreaths their peaks) and part of the Blue Ridge Mountains. It straddles the border between Tennessee and North Carolina. It was officially declared a national park by Franklin Delano Roosevelt in 1940. The park's 522,400 acres (more than 2,000 square kilometers) make it one of the largest in the eastern United States. It is also one of the country's most popular parks.

The park contains more than sixteen mountains above 5,900 feet (1,800 meters) and a wide variety of altitudes and climates. Predictably, that variety has resulted in great biodiversity, and the park counts 143 different species of trees and numerous types of animals, including black bears.

A large portion of the Appalachian Trail passes through the park, running along the border between Tennessee and North Carolina. Clingmans Dome, which is 6,643 feet (2,025 meters) tall, is the highest mountain in Tennessee and the third highest in the Appalachians. The tower at the top offers views for miles.

Before Europeans settled in the area, it was populated by Cherokee Indians. When President Andrew Jackson signed the Indian Removal Act in 1830, many Cherokee left, but some, led by Tsali, hid in the Great Smoky Mountains. A reservation known as the Qualla Boundary sits within the park today, and the descendants of those who refused to be moved are among its occupants.

Cades Cove, one of the park's most popular sites, is a large green valley surrounded by an amphitheater of mountains that shelter the area, making it a suitable habitat for a large number of different kinds of animals. This area was once a Cherokee hunting ground. Later, Europeans settled here, and historic buildings including a mill and log houses dating to the eighteenth and nineteenth centuries can be visited.

Much of the park is a rainforest with trees that date back before the arrival of the colonists. Indeed, it was that rich trove of trees that made this a prime spot for the lumber industry. In 1926, the U.S. Congress declared this a protected area, as it was undergoing swift deforestation. In 1934, John D. Rockefeller Jr. provided funds to make this a park. In 1976 it was named an International Biosphere Reserve and in 1983 it was added to the list of UNESCO World Heritage Sites.

PP. 184-185: THE PARK'S 522,400 ACRES (MORE THAN 2,000 SQUARE KILOMETERS) ARE LOCATED IN TENNESSEE AND NORTH CAROLINA, IN SOME OF THE WORLD'S OLDEST MOUNTAINS. THE FOG-COVERED PEAKS ARE A PLACE OF RICH BIODIVERSITY. GREAT SMOKY MOUNTAINS NATIONAL PARK, TENNESSEE AND NORTH CAROLINA.

RIGHT: CADES COVE IS A GREEN VALLEY SURROUNDED BY MOUNTAINS. DEER, BLACK BEARS, COYOTES, TURKEYS, AND RACCOONS HAVE ALL BEEN SIGHTED IN THE AREA. THIS WAS ONCE A CHEROKEE HUNTING GROUND, BUT EUROPEANS SETTLED HERE AT SOME POINT BETWEEN 1818 AND 1821. RESTORED CHURCHES, A MILL, BARNS, AND OTHER BUILDINGS ARE OPEN TO VISITORS. GREAT SMOKY MOUNTAINS NATIONAL PARK, TENNESSEE.

ABOVE: A BLACK BEAR CUB AMID OAK LEAVES. GREAT SMOKY MOUNTAINS NATIONAL PARK, TENNESSEE AND NORTH CAROLINA.

RIGHT: A PILEATED WOODPECKER, ONE OF SEVERAL SPECIES OF WOODPECKER FOUND IN NORTH AMERICA. THESE BIRDS CAN BE NEARLY TWENTY INCHES (FIFTY CENTIMETERS) TALL. GREAT SMOKY MOUNTAINS NATIONAL PARK, TENNESSEE AND NORTH CAROLINA.

PP. 190-191: THE SMOKIES, SEEN HERE FROM CLINGMANS DOME, ARE ROBED IN THEIR SIGNATURE FOG. AT 6,643 FEET (2,025 METERS), CLINGMANS DOME IS THE TALLEST MOUNTAIN IN THE PARK AND IN THE STATE OF TENNESSEE AND THE THIRD TALLEST IN THE APPALACHIANS. NATIVES CALLED THIS MOUNTAIN *KUWAHI*, MEANING "MULBERRY PLACE," BUT IT WAS RENAMED SMOKY DOME, AND THEN RENAMED AGAIN FOR THOMAS LANIER CLINGMAN, A GENERAL IN THE CONFEDERATE ARMY. GREAT SMOKY MOUNTAINS NATIONAL PARK, TENNESSEE AND NORTH CAROLINA.

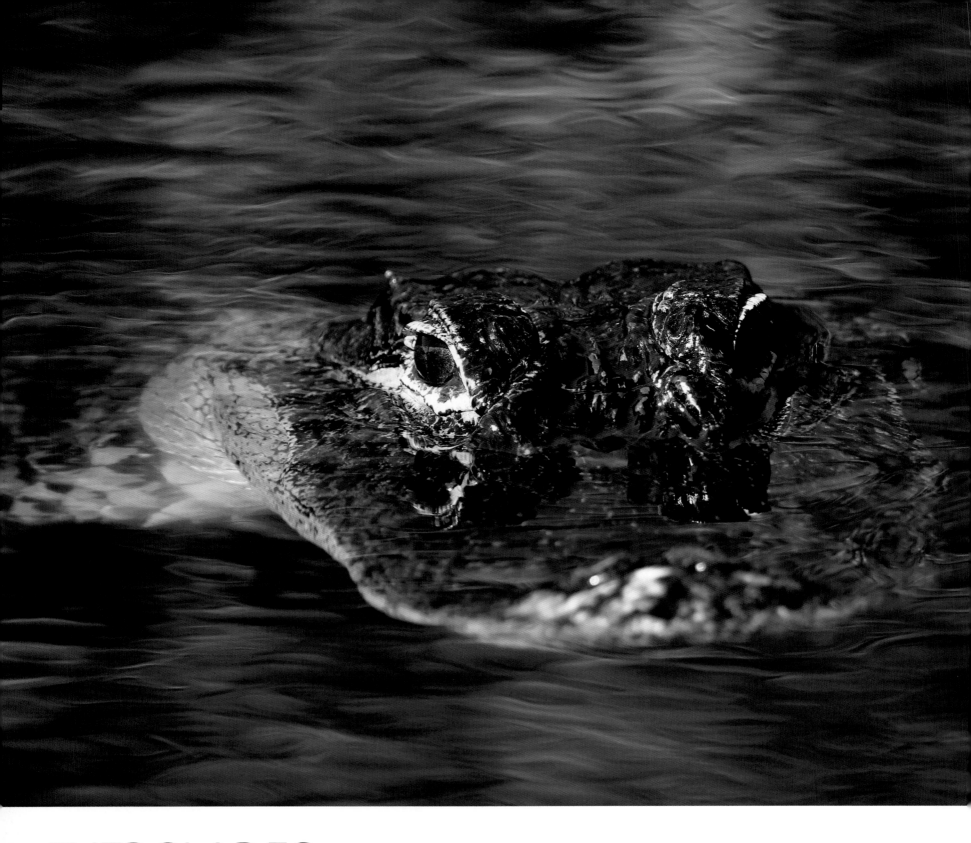

EVERGLADES NATIONAL PARK

Everglades National Park on the southern tip of Florida protects more than 1,500,000 acres (6,000 square kilometers) of wetlands. The water flows north to south through rushes and through waterways—a unique ecosystem that has been designated a UNESCO World Heritage Site, an International Biosphere Reserve, and a Wetland of International Importance.

The area was declared a national park in 1947; in 1993 UNESCO added it to the list of World Heritage in Danger.

The park encompasses just one fifth of the low wetlands formed by overflow from Okeechobee Lake and consists of sloughs, prairies, tree islands, and canals. Many species of birds populate the area, as do alligators, deer, and raccoons.

P. 192: THE LEATHERY HEAD OF AN ALLIGATOR RISES OUT OF THE WATER. EVERGLADES NATIONAL PARK, FLORIDA.

P. 193: THE GREAT BLUE HERON IS A COMMON SIGHT IN NORTH AMERICA. IT HAS A DARK BELLY AND REDDISH-BROWN LEGS. EVERGLADES NATIONAL PARK, FLORIDA.

OPPOSITE: THE FLORIDA COASTLINE FACING THE GULF OF MEXICO IS DENSE WITH MANGROVES, TYPICAL SHRUBS THAT GROW ON THE COAST AND IN SWAMPS. EVERGLADES NATIONAL PARK, FLORIDA.

ABOVE: RACCOONS SEARCH FOR FOOD IN THE MANGROVES. EVERGLADES NATIONAL PARK, FLORIDA.

OPPOSITE: TRICOLORED HERON. EVERGLADES NATIONAL PARK, FLORIDA.

BISCAYNE
NATIONAL PARK

Dense mangrove forest lines the shores of Biscayne National Park. The main attractions at this park are crystal-clear waters: It encompasses the northern portion of the third largest coral reef in the world and an underwater ecosystem that stretches for 100 miles (160 kilometers) in the Florida Keys. Among the many attractions in this area are the flocks of wading birds, and manatees and sea turtles; crocodiles and other marine reptiles live in the area as well.

ABOVE: RED MANGROVES ARE TYPICAL OF THE VEGETATION ALONG THE SOUTHERN COAST OF FLORIDA. THEY ARE ALSO KNOWN AS "WALKING PLANTS" BECAUSE OF THEIR INTRICATE ROOT SYSTEMS, WHICH STICK OUT ABOVE THE WATER. THOSE SAME ROOTS PROVIDE SHELTER FOR MICROORGANISMS, FISH, AND A RANGE OF INVERTEBRATES. BISCAYNE NATIONAL PARK, FLORIDA.

RIGHT: MILLIONAIRE MARK HONEYWELL BOUGHT THE ISLAND OF BOCA CHITA KEY IN 1937 AND BUILT A LIGHTHOUSE ON IT. THE LIGHTHOUSE IS PURELY DECORATIVE, BUT IT DOES ADD TO THE ISLAND'S CHARM. BISCAYNE NATIONAL PARK, FLORIDA.

DRY TORTUGAS NATIONAL PARK

Dry Tortugas National Park includes seven islands off the coast of Florida and some of the best preserved coral reefs in North America.

The park is accessed only by boat or seaplane. It is a natural habitat for sea turtles, multicolored fish, coral, and large shellfish, and it has an interesting history as well. Ships (first with explorers intent on seeing the New World and later with tobacco) often ran aground on these islands. Eventually, Fort Jefferson was built on what is today the park's second largest island. It is one of the largest military forts in the Americas.

The largest island in the Dry Tortugas, Loggerhead Key, is three miles (less then five kilometers) from Garden Key. It offers an ideal habitat for marine animals and takes its name from the large number of loggerhead turtles that live there. The island also has a large lighthouse and the Carnegie Laboratory for Marine Ecology. The wreck of the ship the *Avanit* is found about one mile south of the island. This Norwegian ship sank in 1907 and was discovered in 1970 during an archeological diving expedition.

The crystal-clear waters and abundant marine animal life on the Dry Tortugas have drawn many visitors over the years, including Ernest Hemingway, famed author of *A Farewell to Arms* and other classics, who lived on Key West from 1928 to 1940. This national park was created in 1992, but President Franklin Delano Roosevelt declared Fort Jefferson a national monument back in 1935.

PP. 200-201 AND OPPOSITE: FORT JEFFERSON
WAS CONSTRUCTED OUT OF 16 MILLION BRICKS,
MAKING IT THE LARGEST BRICK STRUCTURE IN NORTH
AMERICA. IT IS LOCATED IN DRY TORTUGAS NATIONAL
PARK, CREATED IN 1992. THE NAME TORTUGAS IS
A REFERENCE TO THE MANY TURTLES (*TORTUGAS* IN
SPANISH) IN THE AREA; THE ISLANDS WERE CONSIDERED
"DRY" AS THERE WAS NO SOURCE OF FRESH WATER
ON THEM. THE FORT WAS BUILT IN 1846 TO PROTECT
THE SOUTHERN COAST AND THE SHIPPING LANES TO
THE MISSISSIPPI. IT WAS USED TO PROTECT THE GULF
OF MEXICO UNTIL 1874, WHEN IT WAS SHUT DOWN.
LATER, THE BUILDING WAS USED TO QUARANTINE
PATIENTS, AND IN 1908 THE AREA BECAME A BIRD
SANCTUARY. DRY TORTUGAS NATIONAL PARK, FLORIDA.

ALASKA AND HAWAII

Alaska, the "final frontier" of North America, is largely an undisturbed paradise of glaciers and snowy mountains populated by grizzly bears, Dall sheep, moose, and caribou. At 663,300 square miles (1,717,854 square kilometers), Alaska is gigantic, and only a small portion of its land has been developed.

For its part, Hawaii is an isolated archipelago, a tropical paradise of golden sand and green plant life in the Pacific Ocean. Volcanic eruptions, surfing, and other warm-weather attractions lure millions of visitors every year, and Hawaii is constantly aiming to achieve a delicate balance between welcoming tourists and preserving its great natural gifts.

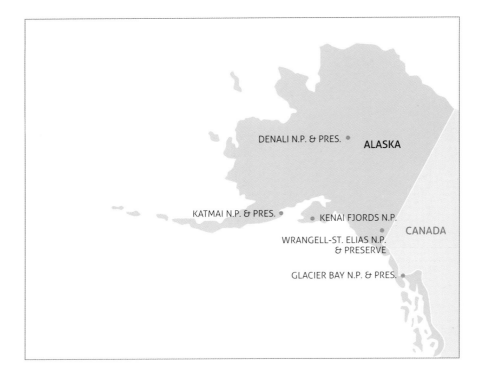

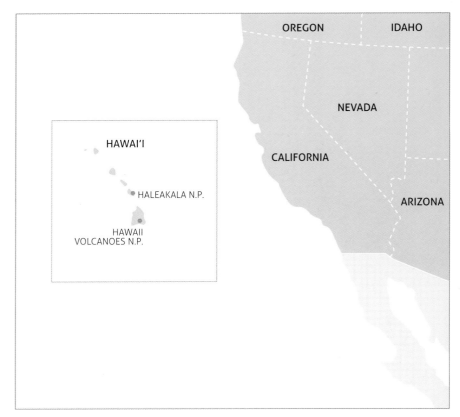

DENALI NATIONAL PARK

Denali National Park, 382,000 miles (614,770 kilometers) north of Alaska's largest city, Anchorage, is definitely a contender for the state's most famous national park. At more than six million acres (24,585 square kilometers), it includes the mountain known as Denali, the tallest in North America at 20,310 feet (6,194 meters).

The park is divided into three areas: Denali Wilderness, where hunting is strictly forbidden; Denali National Park; and Denali National Preserve. Fishing and hunting are permitted in the preserve.

In summer visitors can traverse this enormous park using a bus system; in winter, dog sleds take the place of the buses. There are 167 species of birds in the area and thirty-nine different mammals. The park is known for its large population of grizzly bears, moose, and caribou, as well as wolves, lynx, coyotes, and all kinds of birds, from gyrfalcons to golden eagles. The plant life is equally varied, in part as a result of permafrost; more than 650 different plant species have been logged.

High points of the park include Wonder Lake, which reflects the mountain in its surface, Toklat River, which crosses the entire area, and Polychrome Overlook, which provides gorgeous views of the multicolored rock formations on the slopes of the glacier valley.

P. 204: Massive grizzly bears catch salmon in a waterfall. Katmai National Park, Alaska.

P. 205: Denali seen from Wonder Lake. At 20,310 feet (6,194 meters), it is the tallest mountain in North America. Denali is an Athabasca word that means "the tall one." Denali National Park, Alaska.

Pp. 206-207: The eighty-five-mile (137-kilometer) Toklat River seen here in the fall. Denali National Park, Alaska.

Opposite: A plane lands on Ruth Glacier. The Alaska Range mountains in the background include Moose's Tooth. Denali National Park, Alaska.

ABOVE: DENALI HAS ITS FAIR SHARE OF WOLVES, THOUGH THEY SHY AWAY FROM VISITORS. GRIZZLY BEARS, MOOSE, AND CARIBOU ARE EASIER TO SPOT. DENALI NATIONAL PARK, ALASKA.

RIGHT: ONE OF ALASKA'S THINHORN DALL SHEEP. DENALI NATIONAL PARK, ALASKA

KATMAI
NATIONAL PARK

Katmai National Park is on the Alaska Peninsula, a strip of land dotted with volcanoes that trails off into the Aleutian Islands. Katmai was named a national monument in 1918 in order to preserve the area, which had been devastated by eruptions of the volcano known as Mount Katmai. This volcano is still active today and has an impressive caldera with a lake 820 feet (250 meters) dep. It was formed by the enormous 1912 Novarupta eruption. That eruption covered Knife Creek, which lies below, in pyroclastic flow, magma, and ashes. Knife Creek was renamed the Valley

of Ten Thousand Smokes in a nod to numerous fumaroles emitting steam.

This volcanic park is home to species that thrive in this unusual environment, but it is also a habitat suited for salmon and bears, as well as a large number of different bird species, particularly during spring migratory season. Sparrows, swallows, and tundra swans live in the interior, which has forests, lakes, meadows, and streams—the complete opposite of the rather desolate volcanic landscape around Katmai.

PP. 212-213: A FEMALE BROWN BEAR RETURNS TO FEED HER CUBS AFTER FISHING FOR SALMON IN THE BROOKS RIVER. KATMAI NATIONAL PARK, ALASKA.

LEFT: A BALD EAGLE LANDS ON A BRANCH NEAR BROOKS FALLS. KATMAI NATIONAL PARK, ALASKA.

ABOVE: MOUNT DOUBLAS, NEAR KAMISHAK BAY, IS ACTUALLY A VOLCANO. THE LAKE IN ITS CRATER IS ABOUT 525 FEET (160 METERS) IN DIAMETER. THE WATER HERE IS ACIDIC AND HOVERS AT ABOUT 70 DEGREES FAHRENHEIT (21 DEGREES CELSIUS). KATMAI NATIONAL PARK, ALASKA.

PP. 216-217: GRIZZLY BEARS FISH FOR SALMON IN

BROOKS FALLS. DURING THE MIGRATORY PERIOD SALMON ARE ABUNDANT, AND THE BEARS—WHICH WOULD USUALLY FIGHT EACH OTHER FOR THE FISH—GATHER TOGETHER TO FISH COMPANIONABLY IN THE SAME WATERFALL, KNOWING THERE IS PLENTY TO GO AROUND. KATMAI NATIONAL PARK, ALASKA.

GLACIER BAY NATIONAL PARK

Glacier Bay can be accessed by ferry or by flying Alaska Airlines from Juneau to Gustavus, the small village (population approximately 400) that stands as the only real residential area nearby. Guided tours and excursions in this amazing park depart from there.

Glacier Bay National Park is justly famous for its breathtaking scenery. The snow-capped mountains and spectacular glaciers are stunning. Muir Glacier, the best known of the group, was named for Scottish-born naturalist John Muir, who explored the area in 1879. Muir wrote at length about what he saw, and many became aware of this part of the world for the first time through his descriptions. Great changes have taken place, though, since the days when Muir traveled through what he called "icy wildness unspeakably pure and sublime." Indeed, the glaciers are melting, causing the sea level to rise.

Despite these not insignificant issues, Glacier Bay maintains many intact icy landscapes, and there are many areas that are largely unexplored.

Point Adolphus is a good vantage point for humpback whale watching and offers an excellent view of their group hunting technique. They emit a network of bubbles and sounds that keeps fish immobile so that they can ingest them. Bears, deer, mountain goats, and wolves are frequently spotted in this area. The Glacier Bay ecosystem in the aggregate is nothing short of amazing. For that very reason, despite being fairly difficult to reach, it attracts a growing number of visitors.

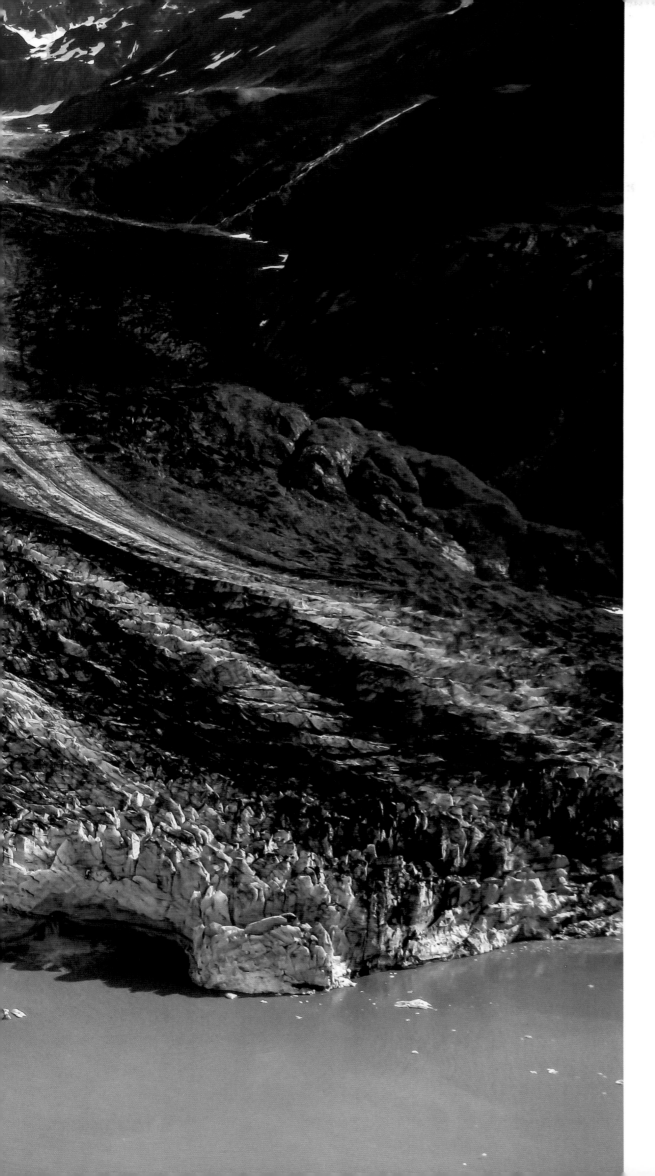

Pp. 218–219, 220–221, AND 222–223:
GLACIER BAY NATIONAL PARK WAS ONCE COMPLETELY
COVERED IN ICE, BUT TODAY HAS SPOTS OF MOUNTAIN AND
RAINFOREST. THE SEA ANIMALS ARE AMONG THE PARK'S
MAIN ATTRACTIONS: SEALS, HUMPBACK WHALES, SEA LIONS,
ORCAS, AND BLUE WHALES CAN BE OBSERVED HERE. MOST
VISITORS ARRIVE BY SEA ON CRUISE SHIPS; MANY FEWER
EXPLORE THE INTERIOR. GLACIER BAY NATIONAL PARK,
ALASKA.

OPPOSITE: AERIAL VIEW OF MUIR GLACIER, THE PARK'S
MOST FAMOUS. IT IS ABOUT 0.4 MILES (0.7 KILOMETERS)
WIDE AND ELEVEN MILES (EIGHTEEN KILOMETERS) LONG.
GLACIER BAY NATIONAL PARK, ALASKA.

WRANGELL-ST. ELIAS NATIONAL PARK

Wrangell-St. Elias National Park was named to the UNESCO World Heritage Site list in 1979 and is an enormous natural park. Indeed, at 13,175,799 acres (53,321 square kilometers) it is the largest national park in the United States. It includes Mount St. Elias, which reaches 18,008 feet (5,489 meters) above sea level.

The park can be accessed via highway from Anchorage. It serves as a key natural habitat for reindeer, grizzly bears, and Dall sheep. The area is so gigantic that it is hard to describe. It stretches from the Pacific coastline to the mountaintops and encompasses glaciers and volcanoes, as well as untamed wildlife.

Tours of Kennecott are particularly interesting. This was a mining town for copper, silver, and gold miners who flooded the area in the early 1900s. The town's fourteen-story mill no longer functions, but it is an emblem of those days and attracts many tourists. There are also opportunities to go rock-climbing and to explore the nearby glaciers.

OPPOSITE: THE TOWN OF KENNECOTT WAS ONCE A BUZZING MINING TOWN, AS THIS WAS THE MOST PRODUCTIVE COPPER MINING AREA IN THE WORLD. IN 1900, JACK SMITH AND CLARENCE WARNER SPOTTED GREEN PATCHES IN THE MOUNTAINS BETWEEN KENNICOTT GLACIER AND MCCARTHY CREEK. THEY FORMED A COPPER MINING COMPANY IN 1906. THE TOWN IS NAMED FOR ROBERT KENNICOTT, AN EARLY ALASKA EXPLORER, BUT THE COMPANY NAME WAS MISSPELLED AS KENNECOTT COPPER CORPORATION IN THE PAPERWORK. THE MINE WAS SHUT DOWN IN 1938 AFTER YIELDING ENORMOUS PROFITS FOR THE MORGAN AND GUGGENHEIM FAMILIES, WHO HAD INVESTED IN IT. WRANGELL-ST. ELIAS NATIONAL PARK, ALASKA.

PP. 228-229: AN ICEBERG IN NAZINA LAKE. WRANGELL-ST. ELIAS NATIONAL PARK, ALASKA.

PP. 230-231: THE PARK'S MEADOWS ALONG THE GULF OF ALASKA ARE FULL OF SPRUCE, WILLOWS, BLUEBERRY BUSHES, AND MOSS. WRANGELL-ST. ELIAS NATIONAL PARK, ALASKA.

HAWAI'I VOLCANOES NATIONAL PARK

Hawai'i Volcanoes National Park, created in 1916 on the island of Hawaii and declared a national park in 1987, reflects the determining factor of these islands: volcanoes and volcanic activity.

The island has a number of volcanoes, the tallest of which is snowy Mauna Loa at 13,679 feet (4,169 meters) and the most active of which is Kilauea. Indeed, the latter is one of the most active volcanoes in the world. Volcanic eruptions have left their mark on the island, from the lava waves along the coast to the violent and uncontrolled flow of melted rock and magma that have reacted to the ocean's waves. The black sand beach in Kalapana is another sign of such activity; it is home to many sea turtles, a symbol of the island's ecosystem. That black sand is actually lava polished by the ocean. As part of efforts to preserve this particular feature of the area, removing sand from the beaches is prohibited.

In addition to numerous campgrounds, the park has more than 150 miles (240 kilometers) in hiking paths. These snake around the volcanoes' craters and through desert and rainforest, allowing visitors to view spectacular volcanic eruptions at a safe distance.

OPPOSITE: NATURE'S TREMENDOUS POWER IS ON FULL DISPLAY WHEN A VOLCANO ERUPTS. HAWAI'I VOLCANOES NATIONAL PARK.

PP. 234-235: BIRTH OF A VOLCANO. HAWAI'I VOLCANOES NATIONAL PARK.

PP. 236-237: LAVA FLOWS FROM THE VOLCANOES DOWN TO THE OCEAN. HAWAI'I VOLCANOES NATIONAL PARK.

PP. 238-239: HAWAI'I VOLCANOES NATIONAL PARK.

Copyright © 2016 Sassi Editore Srl
viale Roma 122/b
36015 Schio (VI)
ITALY

© text, Ester Tomè
© translation, Natalie Danford
© images, Shutterstock

This edition published in 2018 by Chartwell Books,
an imprint of The Quarto Group,
142 West 36th Street, 4th Floor,
New York, NY 10018, USA
T (212) 779-4972 F (212) 779-6058
www.QuartoKnows.com

Chartwell Books titles are also available at discount for retail, wholesale, promotional, and bulk purchase. For details, contact the Special Sales Manager by email at specialsales@quarto.com or by mail at The Quarto Group, Attn: Special Sales Manager, 401 Second Avenue North, Suite 310, Minneapolis, MN 55401, USA.

10 9 8 7 6 5 4 3 2 1

ISBN: 978-0-7858-3627-8

Editorial coordinator: Luca Sassi
Graphic design: Ester Tomè, Nadia Fabris
Text editing: Irena Trevisan, Valentina Facci

Printed in China / SASSI171221CV